THE LEGENDS OF SPORTS

Tiger Woods, Michael Jordan and Muhammad Ali Sports Book for Kids | Children's Sports & Outdoors Books

Speedy Publishing LLC

40 E. Main St. #1156

Newark, DE 19711

www.speedypublishing.com

Copyright 2017

All Rights reserved. No part of this book may be reproduced or used in any way or form or by any means whether electronic or mechanical, this means that you cannot record or photocopy any material ideas or tips that are provided in this book.

The best athletes don't just win games. They inspire us by how they play, and how they live. Meet three remarkable athletes: Tiger Woods, Michael Jordan, and Muhammad Ali.

STARS OF THEIR SPORTS

People have followed sports stars for thousands of years. In classical Greece, the winners of races in the Olympic Games were given high honors and might have a statue of themselves set up in a public place.

Many people become fans of particular athletes. They follow them on social media, learn all their statistics, and think about what they do off the field. Athletes who are really good at what they do tend to have the biggest following, no matter what they do when not in their team uniform.

None of these three athletes got their fame and achievements handed to them. They had to earn fame by shooting the winning shot or throwing the knockout punch. Let's see what they did.

TIGER WOODS

Tiger Woods, born in 1975 in the United States, is one of the best golfers of all time. He had already drawn attention when he was in college and then while playing as an amateur. In 1996 he joined the professional golf tour. By April of 1997 he had won his first major tournament.

After less than a year on the tour, Woods was the top-ranked professional golfer. He continued to dominate golf from 1997 through the autumn of 2004, and from the middle of 2005 to October of 2010. In those months when he was not ranked number one in all of golf, Woods was never far behind.

For a few months in 2009 and 2010, Woods took time off to try to deal with a family crisis. A divorce and other personal issues seemed to throw him off his game, and Woods sank as low as 58th in the rankings. He went over 100 weeks without a tournament win at one point.

Woods regained his form, and his number one rank, over 2013 and 2014. Then he had to have back surgery, and after that lost his dominant position in the game.

However, throughout his career, Tiger Woods has astonished fans and set many records. Here are some fun facts about his amazing golf career.

Woods has been ranked number one in golf for more weeks than any other golfer in history. He has been the Professional Golf Association (PGA) Player of the Year eleven times, a record. In ten different seasons, Woods earned more prize money at golf than any other player.

Tiger Woods learned to play golf when he was only two years old. When he was three, he completed a nine-hole course using 48 strokes, which would be respectable for people who had been playing for years.

Golf Course

Woods has won fourteen major professional golf tournaments, the second best record in history. He was the youngest golfer (at age 30) to have won fifty tournaments at all levels. His overall win count is now over 130 tournament victories.

He won his first amateur tournament, for boys nine to ten years old, when he was only eight!

After Haiti suffered a terrible earthquake in 2010, Woods donated $3 million to help the country recover from the disaster.

He created the Tiger Woods Foundation in 1996. Its goal is to make golf accessible to inner-city children.

MICHAEL JORDAN

Michael Jordan was a United States basketball player. He was born in 1963 and, after a remarkable college basketball career at the University of North Carolina, became a professional player at the age of 21 in 1984.

Michael Jordan Statue

His professional team was the Chicago Bulls, and he quickly emerged as a talented player on offense and defense, and as a fan favorite. He had an astonishing vertical leap and quick reflexes, and brought a new excitement to basketball games.

Jordan, and the Bulls, won National Basketball Association (NBA) championships in 1991, 1992, and 1993. He was considered the best active player in pro basketball, and possibly the best player of all time.

Baseball

Before the start of the 1993-94 season, Jordan retired from basketball. He wanted to try playing professional baseball. He did not do well enough to make a major league career, and so he returned to basketball in 1995.

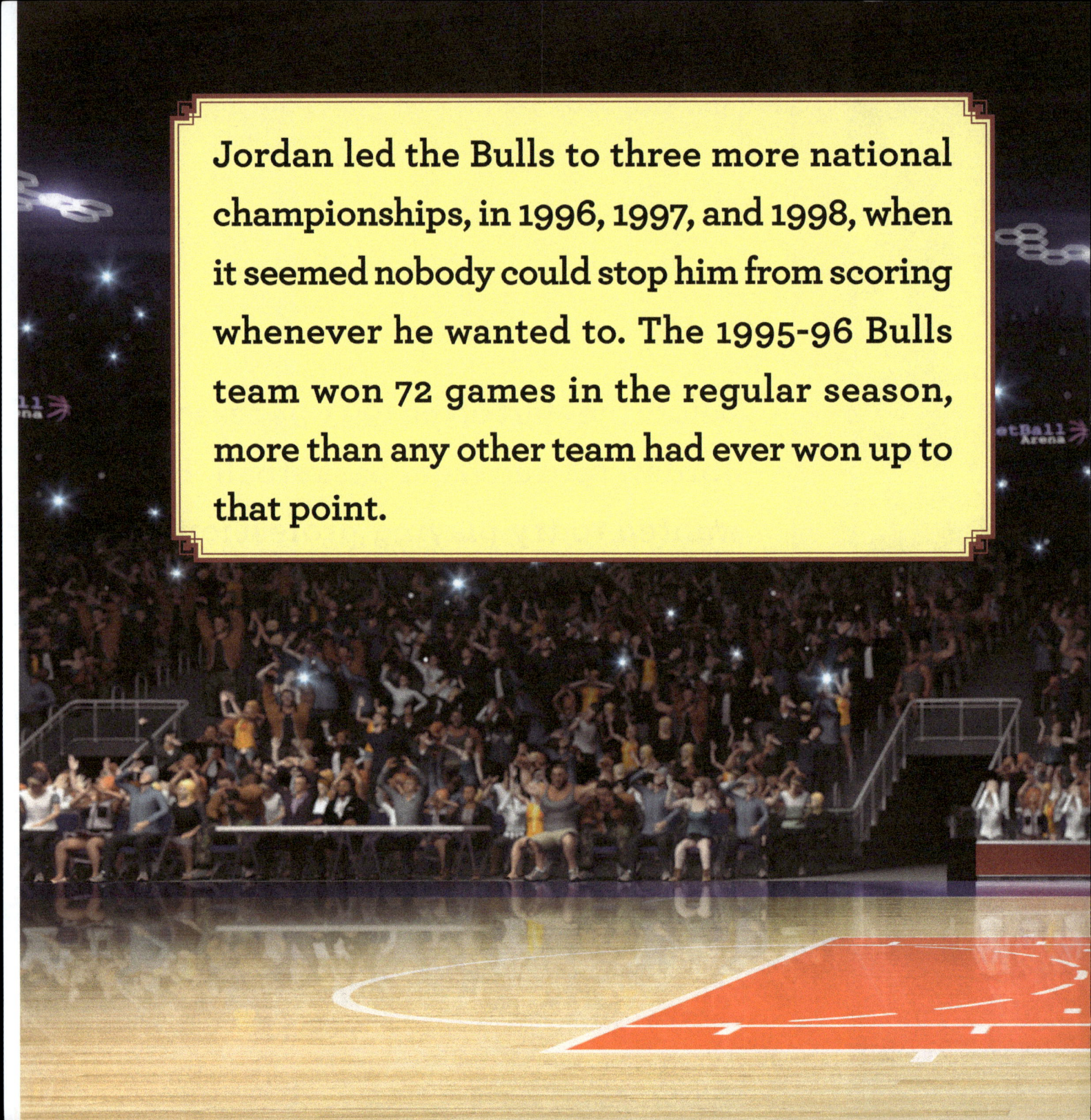

Jordan led the Bulls to three more national championships, in 1996, 1997, and 1998, when it seemed nobody could stop him from scoring whenever he wanted to. The 1995-96 Bulls team won 72 games in the regular season, more than any other team had ever won up to that point.

Michael Jordan retired from basketball again in 1999, but he played two more seasons later for another team, the Washington Wizards. He now is part-owner of a team, and remains active in the sport.

Here are some fun Michael Jordan facts.

"Air" Jordan was the NBA's most valuable player (MVP) in five different seasons.

He appeared in fourteen NBA All-Star games, winning the MVP award for the game three times.

Jordan holds the record for the highest scoring average during a regular season, at more than thirty points per game. His average for post-season games is over thirty-three points per game, another record!

Michael Jordan is counted among the greatest athletes of all time, in any sport. He lands among the top five in anyone's list of the top athletes of the twentieth century.

Although he was always a natural player, Michael Jordan did not make his high school varsity team in his sophomore year. He later led that team to a state championship.

In 1984, at age 21, Jordan was part of the U.S. men's basketball team at the Los Angeles Olympics. The team won the gold medal. He won another gold medal at the Olympics in 1992 in Barcelona.

MUHAMMAD ALI

Muhammad Ali, a famous United State boxer, was named Cassius Clay when he was born in 1942. He grew up to be an excellent and colorful boxer, winning many trophies and titles and bringing new fans to the sport. He was also a social activist, a campaigner against the racist culture that made it harder for non-white Americans to succeed, and sometimes even survive, in the United States at the time.

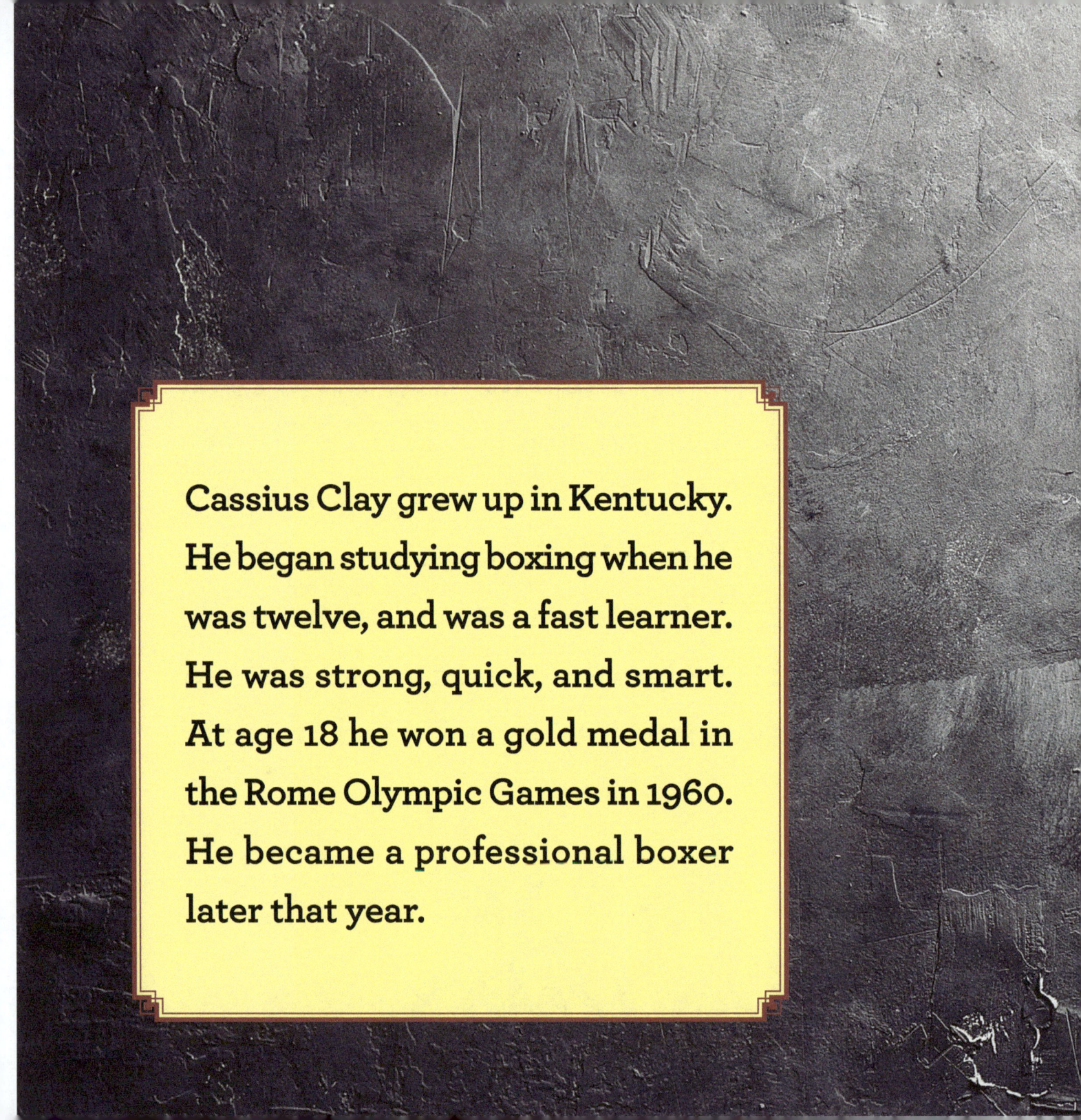

Cassius Clay grew up in Kentucky. He began studying boxing when he was twelve, and was a fast learner. He was strong, quick, and smart. At age 18 he won a gold medal in the Rome Olympic Games in 1960. He became a professional boxer later that year.

Boxing Gloves

In 1964, when he was 22, Clay took the heavyweight title away from Sonny Liston in a match nobody expected him to win.

Soon after, Clay converted to Islam. He took a new name, Muhammad Ali, leaving what he called his "slave name" behind. This was a huge positive moment for the African American community, but very upsetting for many white Americans. There was still a presumption in the United States that people of color who did not "know their place" were troublemakers.

The great Mosque of Muhammad Ali

In 1966, Ali was drafted into the United States military. He refused to report for duty, partly for religious reasons and partly because he opposed the United States' role in the Vietnam War. He was found guilty of draft evasion and had his boxing title taken away. Eventually, in 1971, the United States Supreme Court supported his appeal and overturned his conviction. However, he had not been able to box for four years when he would have been at his prime. His willingness to take a stand for his beliefs, even though it cost him personally and professionally, made Muhammad Ali a hero to many Americans of all races.

Muhammad Ali was one of the best heavyweight boxers of the twentieth century, and many considered him one of the greatest athletes of any sport. He won the heavyweight championship in 1964, 1974, and 1978.

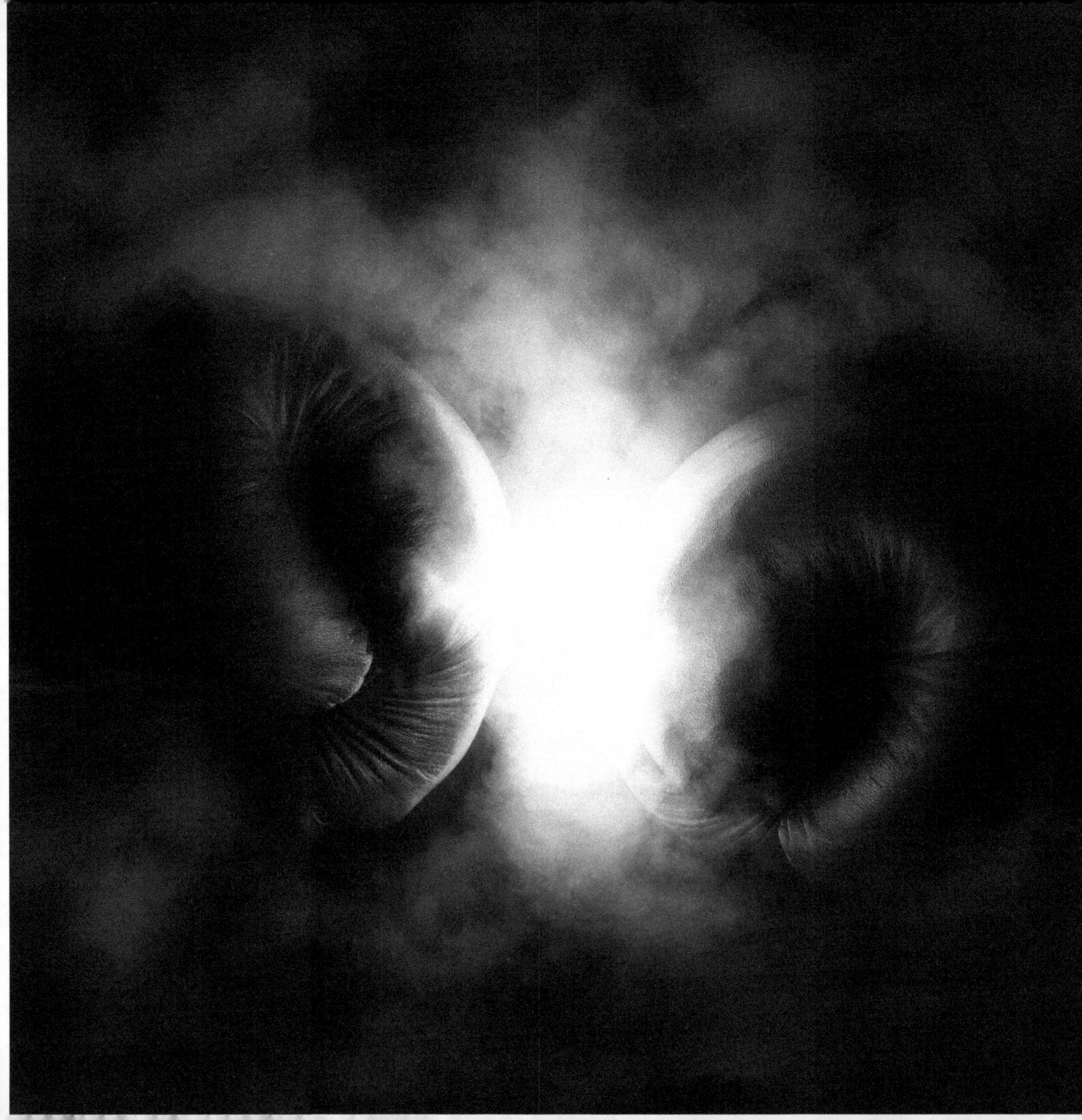

Ali is the only boxer to have been named Fighter of the Year by Ring Magazine six times.

Muhammad Ali was a fan favorite. He recited poetry at the weigh-in sessions, danced around his dogged opponents, and delighted huge audiences with fancy footwork and lightning hands.

When Cassius Clay was twelve, in 1954, someone stole his bicycle. He reported it to the police and officer Joe Martin got the upset boy involved in a boxing program. Only six weeks later, Clay won his very first match.

After retiring as a boxer in 1981, Muhammad Ali spent his time, and much of his money, on charitable and religious projects. In 1984 he discovered he was suffering from Parkinson's syndrome, a result of brain injuries from the many times he was hit in the head during boxing matches. As the illness progressed, Ali retired from public life. He died in June, 2016, at the age of 64.

TRYING FOR GREATNESS

People start from unexpected places and, by practice, dedication, and sheer refusal to give up, sometimes accomplish remarkable things. Learn about young orphans who found an unexpected career in the Baby Professor book Before FedEx there was the Pony Express; and about a rich young man who wanted to be a soldier and found a different calling altogether, in A Rich Man in Poor Clothes: The Story of St. Francis of Assisi.

CPSIA information can be obtained
at www.ICGtesting.com
Printed in the USA
LVHW060337290422
717484LV00008B/526